Legacy of a Lawmaker
Inspired by Faith & Family

THE HONORABLE
Alma G. Stallworth, PhD

Copyrighted Material
Legacy of a Lawmaker: Inspired by Faith & Family
Copyright © 2015, 2018 Alma G. Stallworth, PhD. All Rights Reserved.

No part of this publication may be reproduced, stored in a retrieval system or transmitted, in any form of by any means—electronic, mechanical, photocopying, recording, or otherwise—without prior written permission from the publisher, except for the inclusion of brief quotations in a review.

For more information about this title or to order other books and/or electronic media, contact the publisher:

Atkins & Greenspan Writing
18530 Mack Avenue, Suite 166
Grosse Pointe Farms, MI 48236
www.atkinsgreenspan.com

ISBN
978-1-945875-53-3 (Hardcover)
978-1-945875-54-0 (Paperback)
978-1-945875-55-7 (eBook)

Printed in the United States of America

Cover and Interior design: Van-garde Imagery
All photos from the Stallworth Family Collection.

For my mother

Introduction

I NEVER EXPECTED TO blaze trails or open doors. My life began rather simply, so simple, I couldn't have possibly imagined that I'd end up where I am today: retired from the Michigan House of Representatives; the founder of the Black Caucus Foundation; and a summa cum laude doctoral graduate from Chelsea University in London.

That's why I'm writing this memoir. A lot of twists and turns, mishaps, and triumphs pushed me – a small town girl who once attended class in a one-room schoolhouse – to reach for something so big it wasn't even part of my dreams. My journey has unfolded in unexpected ways and, for that reason, I think it's worth sharing.

Some of it has been rocky. Some of it has been inspiring. But mostly, it's been a pleasant surprise. I'm not trying to suggest that my experiences were happenstance, nor am I trying to suggest that I didn't put a lot of effort into the goals I achieved. What I am saying is that when I look back at many of my accomplishments, I realize they were a result of my instincts as a mother. They were the result of my own parents who instilled core values and grandparents who taught me to work hard. They were the result of my family's struggles during my early years.

In other words, my personal history sparked within me an intense drive to help people in need.

I walked picket lines, served on committees, volunteered at schools, joined the neighborhood council, and always made sure my voice was heard. Although I didn't realize it at the time, these actions were stepping stones to a future in shaping policy. But it didn't start out that way. It started with me standing up for what's right, getting involved in my sons' education, and doing my part to establish better opportunities for all children.

These were issues I believed in. These were the fires that burned within me at night. These were the causes that, for some reason, had my name, Alma Stallworth, stamped somewhere on their frayed edges. So, I rolled up my sleeves and did what I do best: I fought for change. I tapped into my passion for justice and my conviction that family is the cornerstone, the backbone, the key to any successful society, community and individual. Although I'm best known for my work in politics, I wouldn't be anywhere without my loved ones, my personal joys, my memories, and my secret pains.

Alma G. Stallworth, PhD

Contents

	Introduction v
Chapter 1	My Childhood 1
Chapter 2	The Turning Point 9
Chapter 3	Adjusting To Marriage 15
Chapter 4	Family Bonds and Adventures 33
Chapter 5	From Head Start to State Representative 37
Chapter 6	A Whole New World 45
Chapter 7	The Golden Senior Years 51
	President Barack Obama & Family Tribute Message 59
	Biography 61

Chapter 1

My Childhood

THE SUMMER AIR WAS filled with the scent of cherry blossoms – a gentle fragrance wafting from the fruit trees lining my grandmother's five-acre farm. I loved breathing it in as I ran through the tall grasses and around the large barnyard. I'd visited small, rural cottages in the past, but I'd never frolicked along such a vast countryside. So, this was a wonderful experience. I was four years old and my mother and I had just moved to Des Moines, Iowa.

It was so different for me, a little city girl who was used to the constant honking of horns in traffic and houses that sat adjacent to one another for block after block. Nothing excited me more than spending time with my grandmother and marveling at her cows, chickens, and horses. I would watch in awe as she carefully milked the cows, then churned the milk into creamy butter.

Many years later, after becoming a state legislator who began championing causes ranging from women's rights to issues affecting African Americans and teen moms, I sometimes found myself reflecting back to my grandmother's rural homestead. I'd go there, in my mind, to think and to escape. Those were such simpler times and it gives me peace, even now, to recall them. I really believe that my strength as well as my patience were being cultivated back then. I have a tendency to ponder and an occasional need for solitude.

I get my best ideas when I'm alone – thinking, watching the sun rise or sipping my early morning coffee. I credit these tendencies, this need to go inside myself, to my early years of bliss on the farm. My confidence and determination came later – a direct result of my mother; and my humanitarianism... well, that's a gift from my kind-hearted stepfather. He taught me, by example, the importance of giving, while my mother taught me to focus and stand up for what's right. These are traits that have been with me since my humble days in the fields of Iowa.

Before Iowa, I lived in Little Rock, Arkansas. I was born there to two young parents, Lisbon and Charles Russell. My mother was a native of a rural Arkansas community known as Biscoe, less than an hour's drive from Little Rock. The town's population was under 400 and it had such a small tax base that my mother had to move to Little Rock to attend high school. There, she met Charles, whose family owned a successful construction business that was the pillar of Little Rock's black community. My mother was living with a relative, but for the most part, she was on her own and really appreciated the support from Charles and his family. In addition to school, she held two part-time jobs – one at a small diner and the other as a domestic worker. After her graduation, she and my father quickly married, but neither had the maturity to handle such a serious commitment. They were divorced within three years.

That's what prompted my mother to pack up all of a sudden and relocate to Des Moines. Her parents were divorced and although her mother still lived in Arkansas, her father had remarried and he and his second wife were raising seven children — four daughters and three sons — in Des Moines. Despite the demands of his new life, my granddad was thrilled to see me and offered as much support as

My Childhood

he could. My mother eventually found a job at one of the downtown hotels, where she met Enoch Coleman, a handsome young porter. He was a former college football player who had just graduated from Fisk University. After courting for several months, she decided to marry him because she felt he offered her security and the promise of a successful relationship. Several months after their wedding, we moved to a nice neighborhood in a pleasant, semi-rural community.

Although I didn't mind moving, I was nervous, of course, about starting a new school and making new friends. My fears were eased one day when my mother opened the door and there stood a mailman with a decorative holiday basket that was overflowing with goodies – a homemade coconut cake, peanut butter cookies, fruit, and a seasoned ham. It was a Christmas gift from my grandmother, Fannie Holloway, in Arkansas.

Every summer, I went back to Arkansas to visit with Grandma Holloway in her idyllic, little community. It wasn't as large as my other grandma's farm in Des Moines and she didn't have barnyard animals, but I liked it because I thought it was more fun than the city. We used an outdoor well and an outhouse. I also delighted in seeing frogs and snakes.

Meanwhile, I was adjusting quite well to my new life in Des Moines, and I was fairly happy. But sadness swept over me when my beloved stepfather, Enoch Coleman, was drafted to serve in World War II. My mom and I missed him terribly and fretted until he was dismissed with an honorable discharge two years later.

When he returned, we moved to a rural community in Pulaski, Tennessee, where we shared housing with a friend of my grandfather. It was quite an adjustment because we lived miles from town and had to make long walks to most of our destinations. This house was also surrounded by vegetable gardens, cows, pigs, and chickens. Because there was no direct running water in the house, we had to draw water from an open well, just like we did at my grandmother's place in Biscoe.

Around this time, my stepfather found a job as a teacher at the nearby country schoolhouse. It was cramped and very old-fashioned – with battered desks and uncomfortable benches instead of seats. But I loved that school. I was in the third grade and had to trudge several miles to get there. I didn't mind that either – most days. But sometimes, I just couldn't handle it. I'd get so tired, my legs would ache. My stepfather felt sorry for me and began carrying me on his shoulders every day, to and from school.

One day, after carrying me home from school, my stepdad said my mother had a surprise. When we walked into the living room, my mother winked and told me a new member of our family was coming soon. Several months later, my younger sister, Carole, was born. I was six years old, and elated to see the new baby. She was round and fat with a head full of hair. I enjoyed playing with her and couldn't wait to get home from school so I could tell her stories about what I had learned.

Within a year of her birth, we moved again, this time to Memphis, Tennessee, to live with Enoch's parents. His father was a pastor at an AME church that had a sparse membership. I remember getting bored because the services were extremely long and there were so few young people in Sunday school.

My paternal grandmother, Bertha Coleman, took pride in her role as first lady of the church, a job that, for whatever reason, included monitoring my school work and church attendance. Bertha, who was part Cherokee, was very strict and demanding. I was annoyed by all the chores she gave me – sweeping, washing, and drying the dishes. I wasn't used to so many rigid instructions, and I'm not sure if I feared her or admired her. She was more disciplined than anyone I'd ever met – a regal woman with prominent cheekbones and jet-black hair that was always pulled into a tight bun.

But she was a tremendous cook who could whip up a good meal out of whatever bits of leftovers she found in the refrigerator. I was amazed at how she would toss a few potatoes in with a few spoonfuls of tomato sauce, chop up some chicken and create the most delicious casserole I ever tasted. Her specialties were fried cornbread and bread pudding stuffed with raisins and other fruit.

To raise additional money for the family, Grandma Bertha held a fish fry at her home every Friday and Saturday. Although I was only seven years old, I had to help out. The kitchen would fill up with smoke and the snap, crackle, pop of sizzling fish. But I was right there in the thick of things, boxing up the orders and often assisting with deliveries. At times, I even helped catch the fish. Once, I actually accompanied my parents and some of their friends to the shore of a river that cut through a dense forest. There, with my dungarees tucked inside my rubber boots, I watched quietly as my parents tried to master their friends' intricate fish netting skills. This technique required dropping a net into the river and catching multiple fish at one time. My parents tried several times – to no avail. Finally, after a number of failed efforts they caught a turtle. I felt sort of sorry for the critter, but that night when Grandma Bertha fried it and served it for dinner, I took a few bites. I was surprised by how much it tasted like fried chicken.

Needless to say, those were very lean years for our struggling family. After a while, my parents tired of the challenges and decided to move north to Detroit, Michigan. It was 1941, the height of the Great Migration and, like a lot of blacks in the South, my stepfather had heard that the North was brimming with good jobs.

We drove for hours before finally stopping in Chicago to visit with my Aunt Sadie Russell, my dad's sister. She had a lovely apartment and was glad to see us. But there was one small problem. I had a special friend named Billy, a gray and white rabbit I'd received for Easter. I adored that rabbit and, to my aunt's alarm, proceeded to bring him into her home. Except for brief walks outside, most of the time Billy remained in a cardboard box where he slept and ate. That wasn't good enough for my aunt. She insisted that my parents give Billy to an animal control center. I was so distraught I cried for days.

As we moved on to Detroit, we once again went through the ritual of staying with one of my mother's classmates from Arkansas while searching for an apartment. Finding housing was very difficult because, in addition to a housing shortage, most landlords didn't rent to families with children or pets. My mother thought she had found a place and paid $50 of my stepdad's odd job money as a deposit to guarantee placement.

Unfortunately, the apartment she thought she'd found did not exist. In her naïveté, she took the word of a con-man and made a down payment on a residence she had not seen. When she and my dad went to check it out, all they found was a vacant lot with no designated owner. My parents had no experience with resolving legal disputes and, as newcomers to the city, didn't know where to find help. Consequently, we continued to stay with her friend for several more weeks.

I was enrolled in Palmer Elementary School. Because we were living in shared housing, it was not convenient for schoolmates to visit. It was also very difficult for me to participate in school activities. We later moved to the corner of Warren Avenue and Russell Street and into a flat that was located above a couple of vacant storefronts. Yes, these were difficult times, but we never had to apply for welfare. My parents simply did the best they could to meet our basic needs.

My Childhood

A couple of years later, our situation began to improve. My ambitious mother had enrolled in a trade school, earned a cosmetology license, and opened her own beauty shop. Meanwhile, my stepfather found just what he'd come to the North seeking – a good-paying job at Federal Motors Auto Company.

This represented a new beginning for our family. By then, I was nine years old and enrolled in Garfield Elementary School. I witnessed a number of fights after school among the older students. Out of fear, I made sure I left immediately after class, running as fast as I could all the way home. I wanted my mother to transfer me to Sacred Heart Middle/High School that was a distance away from our home; however, she couldn't work out the transfer requirements. So, I was stuck at Garfield until I graduated and enrolled in Northeastern High School, Garfield Intermediate School.

Soon, my second sister, Ila, was born. I now had two younger sisters and a lot more responsibility. While my mother was working in her beauty shop, I had to babysit, wash diapers, and assist in preparing and serving meals. We also had a dog that I had to feed, bathe, and take outdoors for relief. I was an agreeable child, but I did feel somewhat burdened when my sisters got older and my tasks increased. I often had to attend parent-teacher meetings, representing my mother who had to work late at her beauty shop. Looking back, I realize these years were helping set the groundwork for decision making, organization, and leadership – skills that would serve me well as a politician.

The family joined Bethel AME, a church not far from where we lived. It had more than 2,000 members and provided a wide variety of youth activities. Mother required my sisters and me to attend all services and be active participants. Because I was the oldest, I was the most active in Sunday school, the church choir, and the youth missionary society. By the time I was thirteen, I was representing the church at youth workshops, conferences, and weekend retreats.

At the retreats, I participated in the planning of future workshops, served as a presenter, and read scriptures. Since Bethel was a progressive church, it also offered access to the Christian Endeavor Program, which encouraged young members to reach out to the suburban congregations and invite their youth to join meetings that focused on understanding religious differences, cultures, and races.

Additionally, there was a Christian Youth Council sponsored by the Detroit Council of Churches. I was assigned to represent Bethel at monthly meetings along with other teens from various denominations throughout Detroit. One of our major assignments was to facilitate prayer and read scriptures during Good Friday services at select downtown theaters. The interesting thing is that I didn't feel nervous during these events. It seemed natural for me to step onto the stage, stand before an audience of nearly 500, and recite from the book of Psalms.

It was almost as if every circumstance of my childhood – from the fish fries to taking care of my younger siblings – had prepared me to take charge. Later, when I was named the youth leader (president) of Bethel's esteemed Young People's Department, something deep inside of me wondered if this was more than a title or a passing phase. Was it a fleeting moment? Or could it be a step on a journey that would eventually lead to a lifetime of public service?

Chapter 2

The Turning Point

I don't think I'd ever been so anxious in my life. My mom and I were sitting at the counter of a Coney Island restaurant on Woodward Avenue and I was enjoying the steamy aroma of hot dogs and the hustle-bustle of all the waiters and cooks. But instead of smiling, I was fidgeting and keeping my eyes riveted on the door.

After about ten minutes, a handsome, well-dressed man approached. He introduced himself. My heartbeat sped up just a bit. He was my dad, Charles Russell, whom I hadn't seen since I was a toddler. He was wearing a brown cashmere coat with matching fedora hat, an expensive Longines watch, and the biggest diamond ring I'd ever seen. I was impressed, yet kind of bewildered.

A few days earlier, my mother had told me my biological father moved to Detroit and wanted to see me. I found myself wondering why he had taken so many years to find me, but I agreed to meet him anyway. Although I was only 13, I sort of realized that limited money and great distances can keep people apart.

Still, I was confused. I had a wonderful stepfather. He had never formally adopted me, but he treated me like I was his own daughter, and I loved him dearly. So, as I sat there staring at this stranger in the fancy clothes, I wasn't sure what to say.

It didn't take long for him to win me over. To call my father charming would be an understatement. He cracked jokes, told me how much he missed me, shared funny stories about his job at Ford Motor Company, and asked me lots of questions about school. We developed a father-daughter bond almost overnight.

In fact, we became so close, my mother began to regret that she let him back into my life. For starters, he was a heavy drinker. Sometimes he would stop by the house to visit me when he was intoxicated. He would arrive unannounced and often had a large steak that he wanted me to cook for him. I always obliged, but I could tell my mother resented his behavior. She went along with it because he gave her money and because my stepfather never objected. My stepfather was an easygoing man who liked to keep the peace. Whenever he realized my dad was drunk or expecting me or my mom to prepare his meal, my stepfather simply left the room or went out for the evening.

Meanwhile, I was growing up pretty fast. My church activities were expanding and I was taking on increased responsibilities in leadership councils. I served as President of the Bethel AME Youth Council, and was an active member of Christian Endeavor. In those days, people who lived in the city had very little contact with the residents of suburban communities. Schools were also segregated. Christian Endeavor provided opportunities for young people of diverse backgrounds to meet and discuss religious principles at least once a month. Whenever the youth group of another church was selected, we traveled to their church and they, in turn, came to ours.

Later, when a similar program was sponsored by the Detroit Council of Churches, I was chosen to serve as a member of the youth committee representing Bethel AME Church. This program provided Bible study and conversations regarding our commitments to love the Lord and adhere to His teachings. Members were also assigned to read scriptures during Good Friday Services offered by the Council at local theaters.

I had two additional opportunities that were even more inspiring. Bethel AME sponsored my attendance at a week-long, interdenominational regional conference hosted in Williamsburg, Wisconsin at Lake Geneva Religious Camp Grounds. This was my first time going out of town by myself. The church gave me $75 dollars, which I quickly folded and stashed in a purse that was small enough to hide in my bosom. Of course, I was kind of scared, but I was excited by the challenge.

All of the teens shared cabins and met in the main hall for meals. Participants were from all over the country and many had never been around people of color. I was one of only three black teens out of the 200 delegates. But I wasn't intimidated, because we were being taught to accept religion as the common ground that brought us all together. The schedule provided Bible study, conversations about racial and religious concerns, and a chance to hike and play ping-pong and tennis. I relished every moment.

A year later, I had the opportunity to serve as a delegate at a summer camp serving the youth of the AME Church. It was one of many experiences that taught me how to share opinions with others and learn a greater appreciation for differences, whether they were ethnicity, creed, or social standing.

Due to these advanced opportunities and the fact that I attended summer school every year of high school, I graduated at age fifteen. This was a major turning point in my life. It was also frightening. I was adventurous enough to participate in church conferences, but far too timid to handle what came next: entering college before I was 16 years old. My mother enrolled me in Wayne University (now called Wayne State University). At the time, it consisted of one tall building in Detroit's midtown area, along with a scattering of small structures. So, there I was, barely 98 pounds, wandering around a campus inhabited by students who were older and far more mature than me.

Because of my age, I was only allowed to take two or three classes. I opted for Social Science & Math. But on the first day, I had a real challenge trying to find the correct building and classroom. When I walked into the main building to inquire where to go, I wasn't even sure which office would be able to provide me with an answer. I had a schedule in my pocketbook, but it didn't occur to me that the numbers listed next to my classes were an indication of the course number I should follow to find my destination. What's worse, the other students, some black but mostly white, didn't bother to lend me a hand. Most of them were 18 or 19 and I must have looked so out of place.

Not only was I young, but I wasn't dressed as cool as they were. They all had on pullover sweaters, pleated skirts, and the stylish vests that were standard college attire. I was wearing a simple wool skirt and cardigan – my boring high school clothes. Clearly, I didn't fit in.

I was frantic until I finally found a professor who gave me the direction I needed. But that wasn't the end of my college woes. In your early teens, it's hard not having friends and trying to assimilate into an adult situation. I was very outgoing at church events, but Wayne University was a totally different experience. I didn't have the confidence necessary to make such a quantum leap. I was further intimidated by the challenges of college-level homework and research papers that required footnotes.

Eventually, my mother noticed my despair and transferred me to Highland Park Community College, a two-year institution with fewer demands and much smaller classes. By then, I was 16 and found it easier to adjust. I studied there for two years, then returned to Wayne University.

The Turning Point

Throughout all of this, my dad remained in the picture. He was in the background, but his antics – drinking and continuing to expect me to cook his food – irritated my mother. At times, he would give me suggestions about school or tell me what to do. My mother often became angry and would say he was interfering with her authority. She had always been pretty strict, but it seemed to me that she was becoming even more difficult. She became erratic. I was the oldest of her three children, so she expected me to be perfect. If I did something wrong, she would whip me, though she never touched my sisters.

Looking back, I realize that after my dad surfaced, she began to blame all of her problems on her former relationship with him. And she took it out on me. The smallest things would tick her off. My step dad would tell her to just cool out and stop overreacting. But it didn't do any good.

Once, I went to a meeting after class at Wayne University, and I was late coming home. She expected me there by three o'clock, and I walked in around four. She asked me why I was so late. But before I could answer, she jumped on me and blackened my eye. Although I was embarrassed, I went to a Christian Endeavor meeting at church later that evening. When I was asked about what happened to me, I simply said I ran into a door. Deep within I knew my mother loved me, but I was having a tough time handling her occasional outbursts.

Little did I know my life was about to change once more. This change would lead to the independence I desperately needed. A good friend, Florence Evans who was a student at Highland Park Community College, pulled me aside one day and said she wanted to introduce me to a terrific guy named Thomas Stallworth, a college student who also attended Wayne University. Our first meeting was at a dance hosted by the Detroit Urban League. Soon, we enjoyed luncheon dates and visits to my home. My mother was very impressed by his manners and his interest in the family. My sisters also liked him; however, it was difficult for me to decide whether I felt the same way. I was only eighteen, and not quite sure if I was ready for a commitment.

But like my dad, Thomas had a way of turning on the charm. He was also nice, very nice. He wooed me with flowers, phone calls, special dates, and surprise gifts. He never gave up. He had a nice-sized paper route in Southwest Detroit. His customers loved him and gave him big tips.

Thomas was warm and generous. He used to give gifts to my mom, who was still running her beauty shop. When he turned 20 and I was 19, our relationship had become quite serious. Around this time, the Korean War started and he was drafted into the Marines. The following year while he was on leave, we drove to the Justice of the Peace in Toledo and said: "I do."

Prior to his return from military service, I moved into an apartment on Philadelphia Avenue in Detroit. Later upon his return, we moved to Southwest Detroit with one of his mother's friends. The small, upstairs apartment had one bedroom and a bathroom. Once things were more stable financially, we moved to a larger flat on Collingwood Avenue.

Chapter 3
Adjusting To Marriage

I GUESS YOU CAN call it my walk on the wild side. I laugh when I think about the night I went to a new club called the Flame Show Bar that opened in Detroit's legendary Paradise Valley District. There I was, a church girl, stepping out.

It was an amazing place. I was awed by all the women dressed in their finest apparel and the men in snazzy zoot suits. I watched as they piled onto the dance floor and demonstrated a new dance craze – the Lindy Hop. But it was the music that bowled me over most. Etta James was performing, and everyone who wasn't dancing was either snapping their fingers or tapping their feet.

Although I rarely went out, I enjoyed this new experience known as Happy Hour. Shortly after we exchanged wedding vows, Thomas was sent to North Carolina for military duty. I was no longer attending college, so I had time on my hands. Some friends insisted that I join them for a night on the town. I accompanied them twice to the Flame Show Bar and once to a spot known as the Three Sixes. But that was the extent of my night life.

I worked at the church during the day and preferred to spend most evenings in my new apartment. This was the first place I could call my own, and I was so proud of it. It was modern and had a small, cozy sitting area. I used to enjoy coming home from a long day of work, relaxing in the apartment, reading, and daydreaming about the future. I had high hopes for me and Thomas.

I was no longer attending Wayne University, but I had plans to finish college and pursue a career as a legal secretary. Thomas was majoring in accounting, but after he was drafted, his studies were immediately placed on hold. When he finally finished his stint in the Marines, he found a job as manager of the café at Veterans Hospital in Dearborn. The job paid well, but not enough for us to remain in the cute little apartment near the church. We both agreed that it was far too expensive. So, we moved in with a friend of his mom's in Southwest Detroit. It was a rented upstairs space with a bedroom and bath. We thought of it as temporary, and we were eager to find a place of our own.

It took a lot of effort to find a decent, affordable apartment. After a year, we moved into the Brewster Projects, a new, high-rise housing development offering reasonable rent for low- and moderate-income families. I was also pregnant with my first child, Thomas F. Stallworth III, who was born on April 19, 1953.

Nothing could have prepared me for the emotions that swept over me after laying eyes on my new baby. I was a devoted mother, but when it came to being a housewife, I was sort of ambivalent. By then I had blossomed into an outgoing, bubbly young woman. I had grown accustomed to church meetings, conferences, and other related activities. So, when the weekends rolled around, I expected my husband to accompany me to certain events.

Both of our mothers were eager to babysit and often encouraged us to go out, get active, and have fun. Thomas worked two jobs, one at Veterans Hospital in Dearborn during the day, and a part-time job in the evenings. Consequently, our social options were limited. We did enjoy visiting his mother and sharing a home-cooked meal on Sundays. Because of his rigid work schedule, we seldom had other options for social activities. He also attended Business Administration School twice a month in Detroit, studying accounting.

The good news about all of this is that we had managed to save enough money for a used, 1950 Chevy that Thomas drove to and from work. The bad news is that I seldom had the opportunity to drive it because – with the exception of my Sunday church visits – Thomas expected me to spend the rest of my time at home with him.

My new-found independence began to feel like a prison. It wasn't long before we were arguing and I was packing my bags and moved back to my mother's house. During that time, I found a job as a ward secretary at Henry Ford Hospital. Soon, Thomas and I reunited and began living with his mother once again. To my excitement, I soon became pregnant with my second child, Keith B. Stallworth, who was born on April 14, 1957.

One of my greatest disappointments in my marriage was learning that my husband had been sharing time with Delores Simmons, who also worked at Veterans Hospital. Apparently she and Thomas had flexible work schedules that enabled them to enjoy lunch and free time together. My husband often shared this time with Delores on shopping excursions. I knew this because some of my friends saw them together at downtown department stores. Other times, at card parties, some of his male friends would tease him about his girlfriend, chanting, "I'm going tell Alma!"

These weren't the best of times for ambitious, young families. The war led to a shrinking economy and the elimination of countless jobs. Fortunately, Thomas's excellent work performance at the Veterans Hospital led to the offer of a similar job in Hampton, Virginia. I was thrilled at the prospect of relocating to such a beautiful city.

Our move required Thomas to travel in advance for orientation. He also wanted to locate housing and other accommodations. During that time, he made many friends. Many people were very excited and proud to see the first black man hired in a management position at the hospital. His new friends included Alice Brown, a single mother with three children living with her mother. He felt very comfortable around her family because they, like him, were so light-skinned that they appeared almost white.

Learning of this new relationship placed a damper on my excitement about securing a new home in an excellent environment after leaving Detroit. Too often, when pleasure activities were planned, such as going to the park, to the movies, or other social events, Alice and her family determined what we would do and whether we would participate.

Thomas always favored sharing with other people, primarily women. Not to imply that he was a skirt chaser, but I always had to accept ranking second choice in his leisure activities. For example, I secured membership in a couples' club that met monthly to have dinner and enjoy a movie or a social event. He refused to attend, asserting that he wanted to control how he spent his leisure time.

Despite these challenges, I focused on caring for our two sons, especially my youngest son, who had recently been released from the hospital after a very serious illness. Care for him required significant time to administer daily medications and monitor his activities. These duties offset other concerns.

We lived in a small, two-story house opposite Chesapeake Bay in a lovely, tree-lined area neighborhood and an adjacent park. Our first-born, Tommy, attended elementary school on the campus of Hampton University. As I drove him to school and Thomas to work every day, I reveled in the scenic surroundings. But shadows of racism and civil unrest lurked in the midst of our rosy life.

Virginia was segregated – something my children had never experienced. On our way to Tommy's school, we had to pass through downtown Hampton's thriving business district. Every day, Tommy's eyes would light up as he gazed at the quaint shops, the string of restaurants and the city's main movie theatre. One day, he noticed the marquee advertising the movie *20,000 Leagues Under The Sea*. From then on, he began asking to see the movie and, as a protective mom, I wasn't sure how to tell him no and explain why.

It just so happened that I was asked to drive Tommy's classmate to school every day as a favor to his mom. One morning, he overheard Tommy inquire about the movie for, perhaps, the tenth time. His classmate's eyes widened and he repeated something he had been told: "We can't go there," he said to Tommy. "That's only for white people."

When I saw the expression on my child's face, it almost broke my heart in two. Normally, he had a sparkle in his eyes, a glint that, no doubt, he inherited from his dad. But the sparkle had faded, and so had his smile.

"But why can't we go, too?" he asked.

That weekend, I took Tommy and his classmate to a movie theater in Newport News, a city near Hampton. There, we climbed the stairs to the tiny, unkempt "colored section," which was the balcony and the only place we were allowed to sit. I didn't realize it at the time, but a fire was building in my soul. I wanted to be part of the effort that would change things – not for me, but for my children, for my children's children, for all young people of color.

A number of sit-ins took place around this time, and most of them were launched by idealistic college students who opposed the discriminatory practices in retail stores and other businesses supported by the black community. In those days, the stores would sell products to black folks, but not allow us to try on the clothing. To add insult to injury, items of clothing purchased by a black person could not be returned – regardless of the circumstances. Black people were seldom hired to work at these stores either – with the rare exception of a janitor or an elevator operator. Often, we were told to use the side entrance to businesses or not be allowed to enter at all. I'd had enough, and I was so proud to see young people taking a stand.

Oddly enough, many of the older people of color in the community were openly critical of the demonstrations. Although they realized much could be accomplished in terms of steady jobs and decent housing, most didn't want to destroy the so-called progress, so they did not want to rock the boat and threaten their so-called progress.

I got involved in marches, attended rallies, held up signs and chanted, "We want justice," and other mantras that expressed our discontent. But as a mother of young children, there were limitations on how much I could do. Since moving to Virginia, I no longer had the luxury of the babysitting services so freely offered by my mother and mother-in-law. So, I didn't have freedom to rush off to protests and meetings at will. On top of everything else, my husband was reticent. He believed in changing conditions for the better, but he had the same fears harbored by others who wanted to hold onto their job security and relatively comfortable lives.

After a while, I let go of the activism, although I continued to feel it stirring in my soul. Around this time, my mother surprised everyone by giving birth to her fourth child, Merle Coleman. She also began having marital problems. After several years of employment, my stepfather, Enoch, was laid off from Federal Motor Company. Although they had been married for 10 years, my mother wasn't as understanding and patient as, perhaps, she could have been. Arguments flared up over money and they eventually divorced, leaving her with three children to raise. By then, two of the girls were in high school and one was just beginning middle school. Because mother was a modest, religious woman, she always felt the need for a committed relationship. After a short time, she married Adolph Singley, who was also a veteran and had a good job. She later gave birth to her fifth child, my youngest sister, Debra.

All of these family changes happened during the three years that Thomas and I were living in Virginia. Thomas was again offered a transfer by the Veterans Administration to Washington, DC, but he was reluctant to accept the offer because he was concerned about job stability. Instead, we headed back to Detroit and started all over. This wasn't an easy period for us. We moved back in with my mother-in-law (Lucy Burt) and did what we could to get by.

Thomas worked as a gas station attendant and both of us found temporary part-time work delivering Michigan Bell telephone books. Decent jobs were scarce and we both became irritable as we scanned the want ads daily. Soon the stress became too much for us and we began having disagreements and questioning if our marriage was on the rocks. I had assumed he would make time for me and our two sons, but apparently he had another agenda. Rumors and gossip triggered many arguments.

It wasn't long before the boys and I moved in with my mother, Libson Singley. I eventually returned to my previous position as a ward clerk at Henry Ford Hospital. Luckily, Thomas landed a job as a bookkeeper for the City of Detroit. We were so relieved, we reunited and decided to buy a house. We purchased a nice home at 18301 Birwood in Northwest Detroit, a community that during the early 1960s was transitioning from Jewish and Catholic to black. This new social environment required a number of adjustments. Our children were shepherded through the discomfort of a new school, Little League baseball tryouts, and encounters with new classmates – all while getting used to an array of cultural differences. Many of their Jewish friends didn't relate to Christianity or understand why my sons (who were now in middle school) liked listening to gospel music. My sons, on the other hand, learned about Yom Kippur and occasionally attend Bar Mitzvahs. It was a unique experience for everyone, especially me. I had to juggle the challenges of being a school volunteer who provided support for lunch and playground activities, while also serving as secretary to the Little League baseball team. I also was a Den Mother and an active member of the Parent-Teacher Association (PTA).

As a PTA member, I advocated for improvements that would better support working mothers who didn't have time to attend regular meetings and other school-based functions. To enhance my personal time and to better support the needs of my children, I switched from days to nights as a ward clerk of Henry Ford Hospital. This change was excellent because I was able to meet the school's needs during the day, prepare meals, and handle my housekeeping duties.

Throughout it all, Thomas worked two jobs, one full-time with the State of Michigan, and one part-time with J.L. Hudson. This was helpful financially, but I was concerned about the void it created in the lives of two growing boys. I wanted him around more because I felt they needed his male influence. However, he did make sure they took responsibility for manly chores, like cutting grass and painting the house. And when it came time for baseball instruction, he never let them down.

But while his two jobs didn't prevent him from squeezing in time to be a father, they created problems in our married life.

Upon moving to Northwest Detroit, we lived near my dear friend, Gloria Brown. I grew up with Gloria and we both attended Bethel

AME Church. Now as neighbors, we enjoyed sharing time with our husbands, who also favored each other. Her husband also worked nights, which left her with a lot of free time. I had two sons and she had a daughter. We would occasionally share breakfast at Palmer Park, and enjoy a night out at the Twenty Grand, a night club providing shows every Sunday evening.

My husband began spending time with Gloria. They enjoyed private conversations, and made little effort to hide it. For example, during a Halloween Party hosted at her home, the children and other guests were enjoying a bonfire in the backyard. But where were Gloria and my husband? I ventured into the living room, where they were comfortably seated on the couch. They laughed and reacted as if this were normal behavior. I was not jealous; I was suspicious. This feeling intensified later, as she bragged about knowing my husband's food choices, because they enjoyed sharing a snack after he left his night job at Hudson's.

Another time, after Thomas and I enjoyed a night out, he brought me home. Then he left, after indicating he was going to purchase gas. My intuition sensed his dishonesty, so I walked five blocks to Gloria's house. Our car was in the driveway. I knocked on the side door. Thomas cheerfully answered the door! I grabbed him. I mean, I really snatched him out of that house.

Then I got in our car and drove home. He walked to our house, then attempted to convince me that I was mistaken, and that he had just stopped by Gloria's home for a few minutes.

Sometime later, while my youngest son and I were shopping, I discovered that Thomas had purchased a beautiful necklace from Hudson's. I assumed it was for Gloria; he denied it. Furious, I immediately scheduled a flight to San Diego to visit my aunt. After that trip, I resolved in my mind how to manage and overcome the personal challenges in my marriage. I decided to begin pursuing my own interests.

I remained with Thomas because – despite our major challenges – I had a husband who consistently provided for his family, and demonstrated love in other important ways.

Most times I had to attend church, PTA, and community events alone. I had to take it upon myself to connect with our neighbors and get involved in the block club without him. My background as a teen church leader and my experiences protesting in Virginia came in handy with the block club. I knew how to strategize and come up with plans to improve our community, protect it from crime, and unify residents. The block club invited guest speakers, set our own policies and joined forces with other community groups. Our combined efforts as a coalition helped us to raise the standards and quality of life that were so important to preserving property values. Eventually, I was elected president of the Schulze Community Association due to my demonstrated leadership and commitment to further the cause.

I felt as if, at last, I had found my purpose. This was exciting, after many years of marveling at my sisters' talents. One played the violin, and the other was adept at math and science. It seemed so easy for them to chart their future and choose a career. But I was never that focused on a specific goal. I did well in most subjects at school, but didn't have a primary interest. Now, suddenly I knew what I was meant to pursue. I realized that social causes, leadership and even politics would consume my life. Driven to make a difference, I found myself fighting and eventually obtaining approval by the Detroit Board of Education and the superintendent to build a much-needed middle school in our Northwest Detroit neighborhood. The victory was sweet. Many parents had shared with me that they believed their children would have a better chance at achievement if there was an interim period for their personal development as they entered their teen years. It took two years to achieve this goal. However, in September of 1967, Beaubien Middle School was born.

Meanwhile, Thomas was still oblivious. He simply had no interest in civic or social affairs. In an effort to motivate him and spice up our marriage, I joined a couples' club that met monthly on Friday evenings for dinner, a movie, or the theater. This didn't ignite the spark I had expected. In fact, it did just the opposite; he became very annoyed. According to Thomas, he was in charge of his free time and should be allowed to control it without the pressure of ongoing commitments. Needless to say, we failed to build a foundation for lasting contentment and happiness in our marriage.

Yet, we stayed the course and remained in Northwest Detroit for some 40 years while raising our two incredible sons, both of whom were educated at Schulze Elementary and were among the first to attend classes at the institution I helped make happen – Beaubien Middle School.

My mother, Lisbon Singley.

My family, including my mother and grandchildren.

With my sons, Keith B. Stallworth (left), and
Thomas F. Stallworth III (right).

With my husband of 66 years, Thomas F. Stallworth, Jr.

My grandchildren (from left to right): K.B. Stallworth, Misha, Madison (center), Lance, and Joseph.

My grandson, Thomas F. Stallworth IV.

My great-grandson, Thomas Christian Stallworth.

My great-granddaughter, London Stallworth.

Chapter 4

Family Bonds and Adventures

It felt like a bad dream. My youngest son, Keith, had collapsed onto the floor of a gas station near Amarillo, Texas and my husband, Thomas, son, Tommy, and I were trying not to panic.

Quickly, I bent over and pulled Keith into my arms.

"Help," I screamed out. "Can someone here help us?"

A crowd was slowly gathering, but the station proprietor was able to push his way through. He was carrying a small bag of ice, which he promptly placed on Keith's forehead.

"It's the heat and altitude," he explained. "They cause some people, especially those who aren't used to it, to pass out."

Keith recovered almost instantly and we couldn't thank the gas station owner enough. This was our first family vacation and we had planned it so carefully, we hadn't expected anything to go wrong. True, we were winding across the states in a second-hand car that had no air conditioning and tended to rattle whenever the engine overheated, but we had no idea Keith would have such an extreme reaction. After the incident, we checked on him constantly. We also followed the gas station owner's advice to put ice on the car engine.

As for Keith, he was so happy, he barely remembered he had fainted. He was a typical nine-year-old, overjoyed by the opportunity to explore new surroundings. Buckled in the back seat with Tommy, he couldn't sit still and couldn't stop talking about all the wonders he saw surrounding him. It was one of our most fascinating memories. As we continued our loop around Texas, Keith and Tommy were chattering endlessly and asking questions about what was coming up next.

They quieted down when we stopped in Amarillo to visit my grandmother, whom we hadn't seen for a number of years. She had long since moved from the farm in Arkansas and found a peculiar little house that sat on the edge of an alley. In Amarillo, there were lots of dwellings like that, as small as an efficiency apartment and with no space to accommodate visitors.

Consequently, we stayed in a motel just outside of town. Then we continued our loop around the mountains in Nevada and eventually headed west towards the ocean waves and palm trees. We were on our way to San Diego to visit my aunt in her beautiful ranch home just outside of the city. We went to a baseball game and the San Diego Zoo. Later, we rode to Los Angeles, went for rides at Disneyland before traveling south again to Tijuana, Mexico, just across the border. Slowly, we strolled along busy, noisy streets. This was our first time in Mexico, and we all got a kick out of seeing row after row of vendors hawking everything from sombreros, baseball caps, ponchos, jewelry, magnets, colorful ashtrays, and handmade dolls.

I was particularly proud of my husband. Not only did he accompany us on this trip, but he'd come up with the idea. According to his mother, Thomas never cared much about traveling, even as a boy. But he did it for me and, most of all, he did it for his sons. He felt a trip would inspire them and help expand their horizons. To prepare for it, he saved most of the money he made on his second job and set aside at least four weeks of vacation time. I was temporarily in between jobs and our children were out of school for the summer. All of us were ready for this fantastic journey my husband had planned. We had so much fun, and if we could have afforded it, we would have stayed another month.

Back in Detroit, I thrived on my community activities. But my family came first. When I saw how much joy this excursion brought Tommy and Keith, I decided we should travel every two to three years. I was dedicated to my children, and my husband and I were determined to do all we could for both of them. That meant I had to do more than simply give them things: I had to organize my schedule in order to spend as much time with them as possible. My night job at Henry Ford hospital began at 11:00 p.m. and ended at 7:00 a.m. I'd come home and sleep until noon then get up, make dinner and head to the school for various volunteer parental activities. Afterwards, I'd check on the boys in their afterschool programs and return home to put their dinner on the table and help them with their homework. By 10:00 p.m., it was time for bed.

Yes, I was stretched in a lot of directions, but I loved every minute of it. Luckily, my mother-in-law was pretty involved in our sons' lives. She had us over for dinner just about every Sunday after church. My mother, however, liked her privacy, so we didn't see her quite as often.

Oddly enough, my two dads were always around. My biological dad continued popping in to see me from time to time and would sometimes stay for dinner. It amused me, but every now and then, he still brought over steaks for me to cook. By now, I guess it was a bonding ritual. My stepfather's connection was even deeper. He had raised me and doted over me like his own daughter and would always have a special place in my heart.

When the boys were approaching their early teens, I was pleased to announce that he would be living with us for a while. He had retired and wasn't doing that well physically or financially. In the 1960s and 70s, senior citizen apartment buildings didn't exist. My stepfather Enoch Coleman and I felt he would be more comfortable staying in my family's home. We had an extra room and welcomed his company.

Ditto for my sisters. Over the years, both Carol and Merle lived with us at least once, while they were in-between jobs, recovering from broken relationships, or unable to find their own apartments. After a series of domestic problems and a subsequent divorce, Ila began relying on my stepdad to drop her off every day at her job as a lab technician at Henry Ford Hospital. If she felt the need, she also confided in me, and I was never too tired to listen.

Of course, dad was always willing to do all he could. He actually looked forward to driving her to work because it was something to keep him busy and it allowed him to sneak in a bit of quality time with one of his daughters. My other sister, Carol (the harpist) worked as a teacher for the Detroit Public School District and moonlighted as an entertainer at various local restaurants. She has never depended on me as much as the others, but I maintained strong ties with all of them and whenever they were in distress or lacking in resources I tried to help.

To this day, I continue to be thankful for my family and still think of myself as a wife, a mother and... the big sister.

Chapter 5

From Head Start to State Representative

I THOUGHT I HEARD people shouting. I looked out the window; a fire engine raced past. Police sirens wailed. Gunfire crackled. Since I had no idea what was going on, I continued to focus on my responsibilities.

My sons were growing up, and I had resigned from my night-time job at Henry Ford Hospital and accepted a daytime position with a Head Start program sponsored by the Archdiocese of Detroit. As a social worker, I relied on my natural skills to connect with both children and parents who were part the Head Start program, overseen by the US Department of Health and Human Services, which gives low-income families access to early childhood education, nutritious food, and health services.

But, on this particular day, a great deal of chaos was disrupting the surrounding area. I had just invited a couple of parents to have lunch and tour the Head Start classroom in the basement of a local church. As we were preparing to leave the church, the clamor intensified and someone advised us to go home right away.

When I made it home and turned on the TV, I was shocked. It

was 1967 and an explosive riot was sweeping through the inner city. Although this wasn't Detroit's first race riot, it is widely considered its worst. At least 1,400 buildings were looted and burned. Forty-three people died and 342 were injured as entire neighborhoods plunged into turmoil and violence.

Sadly, this meant I couldn't check on the families I was used to meeting with on a daily basis. I wanted to get out and assist somehow, but it simply wasn't safe. I had to keep the boys out of school, and all of us watched helplessly as US Army troops and the National Guard patrolled our streets.

After four days of havoc, things calmed down, and I assumed I would be able to return to my regular routine. I was devastated to learn that my job no longer existed. The Archdiocese job, which was part of the federal war against poverty, was my first opportunity to use my college training and church leadership skills in a professional capacity. I continued to volunteer with the Schulze Community Council. However, in comparison, this was an actual paid position that allowed me to put my years of experience to good use.

The entire staff was so upset that we picketed the diocese downtown. Despite our efforts, they didn't restore the program. However, some of us were asked to develop a volunteer program that was headquartered in the suburbs but designed to set up outlets in the city. My new position included informational workshops, conferences, educational opportunities and travel to major cities such as San Francisco, Atlanta, and Milwaukee. Additional training was provided by the Merrill Palmer Institute, which offered sessions in early childhood education. The pay was good, as was the kinship among employees.

All of the new centers we established were located in abandoned Catholic parishes, primarily on the east side of Detroit. To help stimulate interest in issues involving early child development, I was given the rewarding task of reaching out to the parents of the children enrolled in the program. This effort was important because most of our families were welfare recipients or minimum-wage employees. Many of them needed greater exposure to classroom settings, as well as an understanding of how to interact with teachers. To achieve this goal, I conducted home visits. This was more challenging than I expected because I had to figure out the appropriate time to visit each family, gain the family's trust, and assure them that I was truly committed to improving their lives. I still recall how nervous I was whenever I stopped by the home of one particular family.

The head of the household was a lovely woman with a heavy African accent. She was fluent in French, but didn't handle English nearly as well. In addition, she had a disorder that caused her to fall asleep suddenly and without warning, even in the middle of a conversation. As a result, communication was extremely difficult. I would say something, maybe one word, and she'd say another word. Next thing I knew, her eyes were closing. This would last for a couple of hours, and I felt like I wasn't getting anywhere. This lady (who shall remain unnamed) was a single mom with three children. She was also quite stubborn and suspicious. However, the more I returned, the closer we became. In the process, she began making a real effort to stay awake and speak in full English sentences. As time passed, I was able to address some of her family's many needs. Her oldest child, a 13-year-old boy, skipped school constantly and had been arrested numerous times. Eventually, I was able to get him to understand the importance of school. Both he and his mom opened up to me and began to follow my advice and accept my ongoing support.

I was later promoted to the position of coordinator of the Archdiocese Parent Education Program and moved to another office in Detroit. This office was located in a building that was once a Catholic orphanage for abandoned children. During my stint as coordinator, I remained active in my residential community and continued serving as president of the Schulze Community Council. At the time, we were experiencing a number of problems as our Jewish neighbors began to transition to newly developed suburban subdivisions. This movement also sparked a sudden shift in the viability and appearance of our business district. Shops that had once housed bakeries, grocery stores, pharmacies and fruit markets, were turning into party stores, bars and untidy storefront shops that did not enhance the neighborhood. In order to avoid a sharp drop in property values, the network of community councils, in collaboration with the Detroit Zoning Commission, scheduled orientation sessions that provided us with basic information about the type of businesses that could be prohibited.

We learned that zoning requirements blocked non-traditional and/or undesirable businesses. These requirements could be created by community council presidents or representatives of Bagley, Winship, Fitzgerald, Schaefer/Seven Mile, Meyers/Lodge, and Greenwich Park. Also, proposed zoning changes had to be submitted as proposals to the Detroit Zoning Commission. The proposals would mandate the commission to notify community leaders of proposed new business requests.

It took two years to finalize the recommended change in zoning from B1 to B2 for Wyoming to Schafer – Six to Seven Mile Roads. A petition drive was gaining more than 5,000 signatures that were submitted to the City Council and the Mayor at a Public Hearing involving more than 500 residents and taxpayers. The proposed change in zoning was approved and implemented by the Zoning Commission after review by city leaders. I worked feverishly on this proposal. This meant staying up long hours again and working through the weekend. But it was worth it. Although I was handling the triple responsibilities of being a parent with a social work position and volunteer work, I was determined not to let our neighborhood deteriorate. We were a community of hard-working families who deserved better, and so did our children.

Unbeknownst to me, the local media was made aware of my efforts. One reporter in particular, Don Ball, a staff writer for *The Detroit News*, was impressed by the Community Council's attempts to stabilize the changing neighborhoods in Northwest Detroit. He wrote several articles about our accomplishments. As president of the Schulze Community Council, I was one of the central features. I was humbled by this experience. Once again, I was fired up. Now that I had support, nothing could stop me. After observing my enthusiasm and success, Don and his wife, Mary, encouraged me to enter the race for the Michigan House of Representatives.

At first, I was blown away by their suggestion. I told them I was honored, but that I didn't feel I had sufficient knowledge of the political arena. They wouldn't take no for an answer. Mary and Don Ball decided to enlist the support of the Schulze Community Council. One of my loyal friends and an active supporter of the council began to call me every single day, insisting that I should run. The council was in complete agreement. They said, "You know how to manage and lead discussions. You should do it."

After much thought and a long discussion with my husband, I finally gave them the green light. But as soon as I said okay, I asked myself: What have I done?

I vaguely recall a small voice in the back of my head that tried to convince me to change my mind. Then I thought about the zoning victory. I considered the new middle school I'd help create in our community. I even reflected on all my years speaking and traveling as a teen. I was ready for something even greater, something that would have broader impact.

Don Ball wrote another article, cheering me on, and Mary was gracious enough to plan a dinner for me at their home. Friends, neighbors, and church members came out to meet me. I was on cloud nine. Then the momentum began to build. It seems that people began to come from everywhere just to offer their support. I was getting calls and letters from individuals representing everything I had ever done – my Oak Grove Church family, the Head Start community, school acquaintances, fellow den mothers, childcare workers, hospital employees – everyone I had influenced and everyone who had influenced me. Bethel AME, the church where I grew up as a youth leader, had a congregation that was filled with teachers, politicians, and union leaders. They all rallied behind me and supported my run for the state legislature.

For me, the next step was to cast an even wider net and attract city-wide support. To accomplish this, I had to go through an interviewing process to obtain endorsements from the UAW, AFL-CIO, the teacher's union, and more. It also turns out that my Head Start director, Irene Fogerty, was very active in the Democratic Party. Her endorsement and work on my behalf were invaluable.

But, this was just the beginning. I also had to walk door to door. I'm pleased to say that my husband was right alongside me most evenings. He also worked the polls on election day.

My son, Tommy, was in high school and Keith was in middle school. Yet, the two of them, along with their buddies (including my godson, Michael Matthews) seemed to really get a kick out of putting up lawn signs and roaming through the district, spreading the word about my campaign.

We placed literature in screen doors, mailboxes and, if people were home, we'd knock on the door and chat about my candidacy. It was a tedious and tiring experience. We walked from Livernois to Greenfield, to Puritan and Eight Mile, meeting and greeting people along the way.

We often did this in the dark when my sons got out of school and I got off work. During this hectic period, I left the social worker job to become director of a child care center in River Rouge. It was tough because I was usually up late campaigning and had to report to work the next morning between the hours of 7:00 a.m. until 6:00 p.m. I was required to open up the center, which was located in the basement of a church that held Bible study every Wednesday evening. When we finished for the day, we had to move our desks, chairs, and assorted instructional objects so they would have space.

The drive back and forth was lengthy, costly, and time consuming. Because of it, I accepted a job running a daycare center in Oak Grove AME Church, which was much closer to my home. The center was fully staffed and had the support of a board of directors. It was like a load had been lifted. I now had the freedom to campaign in the evenings and on weekends. And that is exactly what I did. As soon as I left work, I'd hit the trail for hours.

I continued at this pace until that final night. On Tuesday, August 4th, I came home exhausted from working the polls, transporting voters to the polls, and carting food and beverages out to those who worked the polls with me. I walked in the door, took a shower, and stumbled into bed.

At 3:00 a.m. the phone rang, awakening me out of a sound sleep. It was a staff person from the city clerk's office calling to say they had finished counting the ballots.

I WON!!!

Chapter 6
A Whole New World

ON JAN 5, 1972, the entire family piled into my husband's shiny, black Buick and headed to Lansing. It had to be one of the coldest nights of the year. A snowstorm was raging and the temperature was hovering somewhere near 20 degrees. But, my swearing-in ceremony was being held in the state capitol and no one – not my mother, my mother in–law, my husband, nor my sons – had any intention of missing it.

A bold new world loomed before me and it was going to affect all of us in one way or another. Especially me. I was embarking on a path I had never traveled. I would find new causes to champion, occasional news interviews, victories, disappointments, and the struggle of blending the demands of parenting with the duties of an elected official.

Granted, I'd never been a true stay-at-home mom. But now, I was about to become what some might call a never-at-home mom. Being a state representative meant I would have to live in Lansing all week and return to Detroit only on the weekends, holidays, or when the Legislature was in recess. Indeed, I was going from being a helicopter parent to a commuter parent.

It helped that my oldest, Tommy, was entering his freshman year at Michigan State University in East Lansing. It also helped that Keith, who was a junior in high school, seemed to be thrilled by my exciting new position. I also sensed that he was toying with the idea of flexing his new-found-independence muscles. But that's what worried me. My husband still worked two jobs, and I didn't want my rambunctious teenage son at home alone, believing he could come and go as he pleased. Luckily, my mother-in-law was more than happy to check on him daily and prepare his evening meals.

So, with our new plans intact, we rode through the blizzard for more than two hours, all the while chattering about the possibilities and wondering what the future held. I'll never forget how it felt to walk up the stairs of the capitol building, then stroll through those hallowed halls for the very first time. Before the entire House and Senate, I was sworn in by Governor William Milliken. Although I appeared calm on the outside, inside I was nervous and had no idea what to expect. The experience was both exhilarating and overwhelming.

After the ceremony, my family and I attended a dinner with the other legislators at the Lansing Civic Center. I was surprised to discover that, out of 110 members of the House of Representatives, only six of them were black women. What's even more surprising is that the black women outnumbered white women as well as black men. At the time of my election, only two white women and five black men were serving as state representatives.

Clearly, I had a lot of barriers to transcend and walls to break down. I knew that, as one of a handful of African Americans, I would have to work long hours and fight the good fight.

I was so pleased to know that my husband was behind me 100 percent. Throughout the campaign, he'd been in my corner and he continued to offer the same level of support. The day I left for my first official week in Lansing, he surprised me with two going away gifts: a brand new Bible and a clock radio.

A Whole New World

I laugh now when I think about how much I relied on those items. I was renting a room in Lansing Towers, a motel three blocks from the capitol. The facility provided sheets and towels, and I was expected to take all of my belongings home every weekend. As a result, my quarters were sparse. That radio and Bible were among my few cherished personal possessions. On many evenings, I turned to scripture for comfort and spiritual guidance. As for the radio, well, I needed its alarm to wake me after long nights of research. I needed the news programs for current events. I also needed relaxing music and a bit of background noise. Don't forget, I was accustomed to being in a house with two growing boys.

From this point forward, my life was filled with legislative hearings, committee meetings, and public policy issues. I wanted to learn as much as I could about protocol, Michigan laws, and children's issues. My first success was the introduction of Public Act 119, a child care licensing bill that established guidelines in terms of space, staff training, and student enrollment limits for daycare centers. It took me two years to get this bill passed, but I learned a great deal in the process.

Next, I put all of my energy into addressing the infant mortality rate among black infants, particularly in urban communities. When I was elected, low-birthweight babies were common in Detroit. In the early 1970s, 59 percent of the premature or low birthweight babies died. According to a friend, Emily Palmer, director of the Lula Belle Stewart Center for Teen Mothers, many teens hid their pregnancies from authority figures at school and at home. Consequently, they could not afford or did not have parental permission needed to access prenatal care. It pained me to think of all the young ladies who were being neglected. I was especially worried about all the malnourished, low-birthweight babies they were bringing into the world.

I went to Lansing with the intention to fix this problem. I wrote a bill that eliminated the need for parental approval and made it easier for teen moms to secure the care they needed. No words can describe the joy that surged through me the moment that this legislation was passed and signed by the governor. I knew then and there that running for state representative was one of the best decisions I'd ever made.

The results of the bill were staggering. Within a few years, the rate of premature infants began to decline. By 2010, the mortality rate had dropped 64 percent. I was ecstatic. But in my zeal to shake things up even more, I made an unsuccessful run for the Senate in 1974. Looking back, I now realize it was bad timing and a bit of an overreach for me to run for Senate so soon after landing a seat in the House (even though I lost by only 179 votes). To get myself back on track, I left Lansing and returned to Detroit. During that period, I worked for Mayor Coleman Young but, after four years, I couldn't resist the temptation to jump back into the legislative arena.

In 1980, I became a state representative once again and was elected chair of the Michigan Legislative Black Caucus four years later. As chairwoman, I created the Black Caucus Foundation, a non-profit that sponsored programs to boost the number of staff members of color at the state capitol. The interesting thing about these programs is that they seemed to have a ripple effect. One program would lead to another, and then another.

For instance, the Foundation launched an internship program to recruit black college students. One of the graduate students attending Wayne State University wrote a research paper on "Michigan's Response to Substance Abuse." Its recommendations indicated a need for more prevention programs targeting middle and high school students. Based on the research and recommendations, the BCF Board of Directors agreed to support a pilot program known as Drug Free Youth in Detroit. The Drug Free Youth program established a peer group that raised awareness about substance abuse. The peer group eventually developed personal empowerment programs and groups that focused on leadership, advocacy, and academic improvement.

I worked nonstop, both in Lansing and Detroit. Under the Foundation, I had also launched a Teen Parent Program. During my rare free time at home, I was either taking teens to church, speaking to teens and young adults at women's health conferences, presenting resolutions at special events, or attending receptions on behalf of the Black Caucus.

These hectic times were some of the most rewarding years of my life – especially when I was able to squeeze in time for family. My mother was no longer doing hair and had found a job at Herman Kiefer Health Clinic. Thomas, the boys, and I still enjoyed Thanksgiving dinner at my mom's house, just like we always had. And we still got together for Sunday dinner at my mother-in-law's house as often as possible.

No, it wasn't exactly like the early years, but we tried our best despite our haphazard schedules. By now, both boys were in college pursuing their own interests, and my activities were too helter-skelter for me to commit to all the things we used to do as a family. I was spending so much time in Lansing, I decided to buy a house there. That seemed so much more practical than paying monthly fees for lodging. When I discovered I couldn't maintain it, my oldest son, Tommy, who had not yet graduated from MSU, moved out of the dormitory and into the home I abandoned. Then I happily selected a nice studio apartment.

Throughout it all, I was content, and so were my children. Well, most of them. The more I worked with youth, the more I began to feel as if I had emotionally adopted them. My circle expanded, and so did the Black Caucus Foundation. Our Teen Parent program, a project so dear to my heart, grew like wildfire. The Foundation, in collaboration with several child care agencies (foster and adoption), began hosting annual teen parent conferences that included workshops on responsible parenting, nutrition, health, job readiness and educational training. These conferences were held at Wayne State University, and although I never received an official grant, I was able to keep them going for at least 10 years.

Meanwhile, the youth in our drug-free programs were participating in oratorical contests, community service, anti-drug rap competitions, photography, and more. In the mid 1980s, the Foundation was sending more than 100 local teens to the National Drug Free Conference. Sponsored by a different city each year, the conference attracted more than 10,000 teens annually.

These wonderful surrogate children went on to do amazing things. One became a lawyer, one joined the Lansing Police Department, while another is now a public school teacher, and yet another became a Michigan State University student intern to Sheila, Japan. The Drug Free Youth Program, along with the myriad of other programs launched by the Caucus, are proof of something I have always believed: our young people, our neighborhoods, and our schools are like flowers. All they need is support, nurturing, and an ongoing shower of love.

Chapter 7
The Golden Senior Years

WHILE I WAS IMMERSED in the hubbub of political activity, my children's lives transformed. A few years after I was elected, Tommy graduated from college and married his longtime sweetheart, a beautiful girl named Sharon. She was precious and I loved her the way I imagine my mother-in-law loved me.

As always, I was devoted to my work. But nothing could tear me away from my sons and their day-to-day concerns. No matter how busy I was, I remained involved in their lives. I guess I was considered what is fondly known as a "snow plow parent," one of those fiercely protective mothers or fathers who are always in the mix, getting involved, and offering advice.

If you ask me, parents don't do that enough. When your children grow up, they need you almost as much as they needed you when they were young. That's what I told myself anyway. I'm a quintessential family person and I needed to know how my son and his new wife were getting along, what was going on in their jobs and, finally, whether or not they needed my assistance.

As it turns out, they didn't. So, my legislative agenda continued to take center stage. That is, until I received the wonderful news: my first grandchild, Thomas IV, was born. I know all grandparents feel this way, so please humor me as I make the next statement: he was the world's smartest and cutest baby. Tommy (my son, who is Thomas III) moved to Detroit's Rosedale Park neighborhood with his wife and child and, and whenever I drove to the city from my office in Lansing, I couldn't wait to babysit. I loved taking little Thomas IV to the park, teaching him his numbers, and buying him gifts.

Before long, I was blessed with a second grandson, his brother Joseph. The stories I have about these two would fill several books. My favorite memory of Joseph is his fourth birthday when he became so excited, he thrust his entire head into his birthday cake. What a mess he made! But it was a fun mess. After we got over our shock, we doubled over with laughter.

You see, I didn't grow up with brothers, so I wasn't used to all the shenanigans and, believe me, Joseph and Tommy IV kept us on our toes. Once, Joseph nearly scared us to death. Without us knowing it, he had climbed out on the upstairs porch and tried to imitate Superman. Fortunately, his dramatic leap to the ground thirty feet below didn't leave him with broken bones or any other injuries.

The same applies to Tommy IV. I used to hold my breath whenever "Knock 'em Down Stallworth" (as he was called by his coach) appeared on the football field and made one of his high-speed dashes. He was an outstanding football player for U of D Jesuit High School, earning an athletic scholarship that enabled him to enroll in Florida A&M University.

Because I was heavily involved in my political career, I didn't get as much time as I would have liked with my grandsons. However, when the third grandchild, Misha, was born, the heavens opened up. By then I had a little more flexibility in my schedule and, of course, I was anxious to spend it with my very first granddaughter. On her first

Christmas, she amazed everyone by clapping her chubby little hands every time she unwrapped a present. Before she entered preschool, she was already getting into mischief and proving that while she may have looked like an adorable china doll, she was as much a daredevil as her brothers. She scrambled up the stairs, climbed trees, and slid down boulders whenever she got the chance.

In some ways, she seemed to bring the family closer together. We attended Thanksgiving Day parades, visited Santa, and went to a host of dinners at the homes of the great-grandparents (my mother and mother-in-law). Even though my work continued to keep me busy, I was finding ways to squeeze in time with my grandchildren during Legislative Conferences held in Florida, California, and northern Michigan. While in Florida and California, they accompanied me to Disney World as well as the zoo and SeaWorld. Grandfather Thomas (whom they called Pops) babysat while I attended meetings.

My son, Thomas III and his wife Sharon, did an excellent job raising their children. All are outstanding young people who never gave up on their dreams.

Tommy IV became a Naval flyer after graduating from Florida A&M and graduating from Officer Training School.

Joseph completed undergraduate studies at Michigan State University, graduated from Chicago Law School, and is now a practicing attorney.

Misha graduated from the University of Chicago, and the University of Michigan School of Social Work and worked for a while as a social worker for the Detroit Area Office of Aging, Inc. She's also the first grandchild to follow in my footsteps. Brilliant and energetic, she ran for public office while still in her twenties. In November of 2016, she was elected to the Detroit Community School Board. She ran a strategic and dynamic campaign that reminded me of my first efforts to get elected. It all paid off, and I'm as proud of her as I am of all my children and grandchildren.

But I've had to take the bitter with the sweet. Although the senior years helped me carve out more time for grandchildren, they also have meant saying goodbye to many who have been in my life for years. As I grew older, my parents' health began failing. My biological father died during my middle age years and my mother, who had suffered from congestive heart disease, had a heart attack about 10 years later. My stepfather lived longer than either of my parents. After residing at my home for a while, he had a strong yearning to move back to Kentucky. He lived there in solitude in a house on a plot of land that he owned. Although it must have been lonely, it was peaceful and it was what he wanted. Soon after moving there, he died one night in his sleep.

Around this time, I retired from the House of Representatives and began pursuing degrees online by enrolling at Chelsea University in London, England. I had already finished my bachelor's degree, but I also wanted a master's degree and PhD. I didn't need the degrees to fulfill any obligations. I did it for me. I'd always had the desire to complete my education, and I thought it was a great way to invest my time. I delved in with enthusiasm, taking classes in health sciences, law, public health management, and public health education. Between 1975 and 1992, I earned a Bachelor of Science degree; a Master of Arts in Health Promotion and Education; and a PhD in Administration Business and Nonprofits.

By the time I had finished my courses, my health was beginning to decline. As the years advanced, I began developing little aches and pains. Unfortunately, this meant making adjustments in my diet, lifestyle, and career. After I went into full retirement, and it seemed like suddenly, time was moving very slowly. I was dealing with a hiatus in my life. I felt as if I were at a standstill.

When I reached out to others, they tried, but couldn't always be there. They had jobs, commitments, and meetings to attend. I began to realize that, for nearly everyone else, the clock was ticking swiftly and the hours were marching forward at the same speed. It dawned on me that the world was turning at the same fast pace. I concluded, then and there, that I was the one who was slowing down, and I probably wouldn't be able to get ongoing, round-the-clock support from family. My adult children were consumed with their individual careers, problems, and personal goals. Clearly, they wanted to devote more of their time to me. But it wasn't always possible, especially since they had families and demanding occupations.

Both of my sons have served in public office. Thomas III was elected as State Representative in 2011. (He remarried several years ago and his wife, Nikki, is Vice President of Oakland University in Rochester, Michigan). Keith was elected to the Michigan House of Representatives in 1977. Unlike his brother, he and his wife, Nicole T. Stallworth, Executive Director of the Black Caucus Foundation of Michigan, started a family after I retired.

That was good news for me, because I love spending time with my eight grandchildren, including Keith and Nicole's newborn son, Harrison, and their three children, Lance, Madison, and Keith Jr., who received a full scholarship to attend Michigan State University.

My youngest grandchildren never cease to amaze me. At age six, Madison was elected a member of the student council at her elementary school. In preparation for the campaign, she developed posters and special announcements, and gave introductory speeches. At age eight, she discovered her special talents in art, making jewelry and other items which she sells to family and friends. I have to admit, they have stimulated a great joy in me as a senior citizen. I have taken advantage of opportunities to share in special school programs, plays, concerts, and art exhibits, as well as annual birthday celebrations.

So, when I found out about my illnesses, I still had many reasons to get excited: my loved ones are the number one reason. I have a growing family – including great grandchildren. My grandson, Tommy IV and his wife, Asia, have a precocious daughter, London, and a son, Christian, a champion lacrosse player who received a full scholarship to attend University of Detroit-Mercy in 2018. Just like my children, my grandchildren and my great-grandchildren give me something to look forward to in the days ahead.

When you become a senior, you exist on faith. True, you need your doctors and, true again, you rely on health advice and medical remedies. But faith is a major factor as well. I have tackled diabetes, heart disease, and cancer, and I've had major surgeries that have required hospitalization. I couldn't have gotten through this without a loving family and the devout belief in God that was instilled in me at such a young age.

I look back on my teen years and thank my mother for encouraging me (actually making me) to study the Bible and totally devote myself to church and community service. Today, I consider this a major source of my strength. It is my bedrock as I sort through my insurance options and make decisions about specific provisions for the coverage of medications as prescribed by doctors for effective treatments.

I was surprised to discover that Medicare – often touted as the savior for seniors – does not always meet the increasing costs of hospitals, doctors, lab work, and prescriptions. For some seniors, the required co-pays add to the costs and seriously impact their ability to seek medical assistance. As we continue to age, the health issues that require treatment eventually begin to turn us into a drug-dependent population. The continuing political debate regarding the solvency of Social Security is another issue that needs to be addressed by and for seniors. We absolutely must support the leaders, elected officials, and policy makers who have been willing to take a stand and make the challenges facing seniors a priority.

In my case, this won't cause a setback of any kind. I have adequate health care coverage due to the number of years I served in the Michigan House of Representatives. I have also been blessed with a loving and caring husband as well as two sons who have been by my side helping me cope with any illness that comes my way. This is not the case for everyone. My heart goes out to those who have to fret about who will care for them and how they will afford treatment. For this reason, I try to urge everyone I meet to write to their representative in the US Congress, and picket if necessary. Do all you can to fight for affordable health care for yourself and the next generation.

As I write these words I am now 86 years of age and looking forward to my next birthday. I'm determined to be as strong as I was during the days when I was assisting my aging parents with their recovery. But it hasn't been easy. I experienced my first heart attack during recovery from colon surgery.

Later, I was diagnosed with congestive heart disease. My two sons, Thomas and Keith, intervened when it was recommended that I needed open heart surgery. They both felt the recovery would be very difficult after enduring prior colon surgery. Because of those concerns, we sought a second opinion and secured a cardiologist who provided alternative procedures. The new cardiologist's recommendations included plans designed to reduce the chance of heart failure for at least four years. During this period, additional stents were placed in my heart valve to remove blockages that were preventing the normal flow of blood.

While I cope with these challenges, I continue to find happiness in memories of an extended family that I know would make our ancestors so proud. They didn't live to see my children run for public office, travel the world, and move into impressive suburban homes. But they set the stage. One milked cows on a farm in Arkansas. Another taught in that modest one-room schoolhouse in rural Tennessee. And still another eked out a living frying fish in a tiny smoke-filled kitchen in Memphis. Yet they held their heads high and walked before us in dignity as they paved the way.

Whenever I think about what they accomplished, my heart fills with emotion and tears run down my cheeks. They make me proud of every speech I ever gave, every bill I ever helped pass. They are the inspiration and they are the torch I am humbly passing on to my progeny.

That, I suppose, is what life is all about.

President Barack Obama & Family Tribute Message

It has been the privilege of the Stallworth family to support the first and only African American President in the history of this country. He served with dignity, demonstrating trustworthy leadership and a compassion. He is joined by his lovely wife and family, setting a precedence as well as legacy for our children in future years.

Biography

THE HONORABLE ALMA G. Stallworth, PhD is an exemplary leader whose values and policies are rooted in faith, family, and fairness for people everywhere. Born in Little Rock, Arkansas, in 1932, she moved to Detroit, Michigan, as a child. Academic excellence enabled her to graduate from Northeastern High School at age 15, and she attended Wayne State University.

In 1951, she married Thomas F. Stallworth, Jr. and they are now celebrating 67 years of marriage. Their two sons, Thomas F. Stallworth III and Keith B. Stallworth, and their wives have blessed the couple with grandchildren and great-grandchildren as well.

Dr. Stallworth is best known for serving in the Michigan House of Representatives. She was first elected in 1970 and served until 2005, including 18 years as Chair of the powerful Committee of Public Utilities.

She is also celebrated as the founder of the Black Caucus Foundation of Michigan in 1985. The non-profit organization sponsored an Intern Program for college students and founded the Drug Free Youth in Detroit Program. The longtime Bethel AME Church member has also led youth groups in Africa.

After retirement, she became a summa cum laude doctoral graduate with great distinction from Chelsea University in London, England, where she earned a Master's in Health Promotion & Education, and a PhD in Business Administration.

Dr. Stallworth has authored several books, including: her memoir, Legacy of a Lawmaker: Inspired by Faith & Family, and Broken Hearts: Like Mother, Like Daughter, A Spiritual Call for Equality in Health Care.

www.ingramcontent.com/pod-product-compliance
Lightning Source LLC
Chambersburg PA
CBHW030103100526
44591CB00008B/253